mini ENC

# BIRDS

Domestic
Turkey

## Contents

D0053305

# What is a bird?

There are over 9,000 different species of birds. All birds have beaks, wings, and feathers, and most birds can fly. Birds began life over 150 million years ago as relatives of the dinosaurs.

Birds have wings instead of arms.

Birds have powerful muscles that keep their wings flapping. These muscles attach to a large plate of bone in the bird's chest.

Birds have pointed claws instead of toenails.

A bird's ears are hidden underneath its feathers.

Birds have a hard beak, but no teeth. This means that they can't chew their food.

Birds breathe oxygen into their lungs, but they also store it in small air sacs around their body. This makes the oxygen easily available and helps them to keep flying, even when it is hard work!

Blue and Gold Macaw

## Hollow bones

Most birds have bones that are hollow. If their bones were solid, birds would be too heavy to fly. A bird's bones can sometimes be lighter than its feathers!

# Bird life

All birds lay eggs rather than giving birth. Female birds usually lay hard-shelled eggs in a nest, which may be made of twigs and grass and hidden in the trees, or in a simple hole on the ground. A nest provides a safe place for laying eggs and raising young, and some birds will sleep here through the year.

## Attraction

To attract a mate, male birds will show off to females in a variety of ways. The male blue-footed booby bird shows off to the female by performing a high-stepping walk with its blue feet!

## Eggs

Bird eggs come in different colors and shapes to help them blend into their surroundings and avoid being eaten. Guillemots breed on cliffs. Their eggs are long with a pointed end. This makes the eggs less likely to roll off the cliff.

## Hatching

1. Bird parents sit on their eggs to keep them warm.

2. When the young bird is ready, it pecks a hole in the egg with its beak and pushes out of the egg.

3. Until a chick can fly, it relies upon its parents for food.

# Flying

Birds' wings are shaped to suit the way they fly. Eagles have broad wings to soar through the sky, while most forest-living birds have shorter wings to fly from one tree to another.

A bird's wing is curved. This helps it to rise and steer through the air.

American Bluebird

## Flying

Birds fly by flapping their wings up and down.

## Taking off

Small birds can take off by jumping in the air and flapping their wings. Larger birds, like swans, run upwards while flapping their wings.

A bird's feathers help it push through the air. As the wings flap down, they push air back and the bird moves forward.

## Landing

To land, a bird controls its wings and tail and slows down. Then it spreads out its wings and drops gently to where it wants to land.

## Feathers

Feathers grow all over a bird's body. They keep birds warm and help them to fly. There are several different types of feathers, including down, body, and flight feathers.

# Flightless birds

Ostriches and penguins are both flightless birds. Ostriches live on the grassy plains of Africa. Penguins live in the southern hemisphere, and some can even survive the extreme cold of Antarctica.

The emperor penguin lives in Antarctica. It is the largest penguin.

Emperor Penguin

Beak

## Keeping warm

A layer of fat underneath penguins' skin helps them to stay warm. This fat is called blubber.

A penguin has more feathers than most birds. Its feathers are waterproof.

Penguins use stiff, flipper-like wings to swim quickly through the water.

Webbed toes help penguins to steer through the water.

Beak

Loose, shaggy feathers

Ostrich

**Big eggs**

Ostriches lay the largest eggs of all living birds.

The ostrich has a sharp claw on each foot.

Ostriches have long, muscular legs for running away from attacking lions and cheetahs. They can also kill lions by kicking them.

Ostrich egg

Chicken egg

11

# Game birds

Game birds usually have a small head and a plump body. They are not strong fliers and tend to live on the ground in woodlands and hedges, where they can hide easily. Game birds include pheasants, partridges, peafowl, guinea fowl, grouse, and turkeys.

Peafowl have a short, thick beak that they use to eat seeds, small animals, and plant shoots.

Peacock

## Other game birds

Guinea Fowl

Partridge

Grouse

Peacocks have about 200 tail feathers.

A peacock fans out its tail feathers to attract a mate. Peahens will choose the male with the biggest fan to make sure that their young will also grow large fans.

Peacocks have beautiful colored feathers, while peahens are brown.

## Pheasants

Pheasants are game birds that live together in small flocks. The male pheasant has a red fold of skin, called a wattle, hanging over each side of its blue head.

Domestic Turkey

# Songbirds

Most birds sing or make noises, but songbirds are known for their ability to sing beautiful songs. In the songbird's windpipe, near their lungs, is a special voice box called a "syrinx." The syrinx has walls that vibrate as air passes over them. This creates a sound. Songbirds have a more complicated syrinx than other birds, which lets them create more sounds.

### Mockingbird

The mockingbird gets its name because it can copy other birds' songs and sound just like them.

Nightingale

## Nightingale

The most famous songbird is the nightingale. Most songbirds only sing during the day, but the nightingale sings at nighttime too.

# Waterfowl

Waterfowl include birds like ducks, swans, and geese. They have waterproof feathers and live around rivers, lakes, and ponds. Like many birds, waterfowl lose and grow new flight feathers every year.

Waterfowl clean their feathers regularly with their beak.

Male Mallard Duck

## Migration

Some birds travel a long distance every year to avoid cold weather and find food. This is called migration. Snow geese migrate every winter, by flying in a "V" shape. The leader works hard to push through the air and this makes it easier for the others to fly behind. When the leader gets tired, another goose takes its place.

**Swans**

Swans have a large body and a long, curved neck. They dip their neck and head under the water to find food.

Female Mallard Duck

The female mallard duck is brown, while the male is more colorful, with a dark green head.

Like many birds, waterfowl have a preen gland near their tail. The preen gland produces an oil, which the birds use to cover their feathers to keep them waterproof.

Mallard Duckling

Young ducks are called ducklings.

Webbed feet help the duck paddle through the water.

17

# Owls

Owls are unmistakeable birds that generally hunt at nighttime and sleep during the day. Most owls make their nests in trees and live on their own unless they are raising their young.

Owls have a circle of feathers known as a disc around each eye.

Owls use their talons to grab mice, small birds, and sometimes fish.

## Head turner

Tawny Owl

Owls have excellent eyesight, but their eyes can only see what is in front of them. In order to see to the side or to the back, they have to turn their head. They can turn their head almost all the way around.

## Other owls

Eastern Screech Owl

18

Fluffy flight feathers allow the owl to fly very quietly.

Brown feathers help the owl to blend in with its surroundings.

Eurasian Eagle Owl

## Blending in

The snowy owl lives in the Arctic and has snow-white feathers that make it hard to see in the winter snow. In the spring, the owl molts and grows new gray-brown feathers.

Barn Owl

Great Horned Owl

Short-Eared Owl

# Parrots

Parrots are some of the world's most beautiful and colorful birds. The parrot family is made up of over 300 different species and includes cockatoos, budgerigars, and lorikeets. Most parrots live together in large flocks in warm tropical rain forests.

Citron-Crested Cockatoo

Brightly colored feathers help parrots to see each other.

Two toes face forwards and two toes face backwards. This helps the parrot grip on to branches and hold fruit, nuts, and seeds.

## Cockatoos

Cockatoos have a crest of feathers on top of their head. They raise the crest when they are frightened, angry, or excited.

The parrot's curved beak helps it crush and eat nuts and seeds. Some parrots use their beak to climb by gripping on to tree trunks.

Parrots are intelligent birds. They have a large skull, which gives more space for their brain!

Gray Parrot

## Chatty birds

Many birds can copy human words, but the gray parrot is a particularly brilliant talker. It can mimic people and even understand what some words mean. The most talkative of all birds, though, is the budgerigar. One budgie called Puck learned how to say 1,728 words!

Sky Blue Budgerigar

Scarlet Macaw

# Waders

Wading birds live in shallow waters like marshes, swamps, and the edges of rivers and lakes. Most waders stride through the water on long, thin legs and have specially shaped beaks that help them to search for and grab their food.

Flamingos wade through lakes on their long legs. They also use their legs to stir up the water before feeding.

Webbed feet

Flamingos have a curved, upside-down beak. They feed by taking in water and sieving out any small water creatures through their beak.

## Curlews

The curlew uses its long, curved beak to find worms in the mud.

Flamingos get their bright pink color from the food they eat. Young flamingos are white and gray when they hatch.

Lesser Flamingo

## Herons

Herons are excellent fishers. They stand and wait patiently for hours until a fish comes towards them. Once a fish is near, the heron stabs and swallows it whole. Herons also eat insects, frogs, and small mammals.

# Birds of prey

With their sharp beak and talons, amazing eyesight, and the ability to speed through the air, birds of prey are the expert hunters of the sky. Birds of prey are also called raptors and include birds like eagles, buzzards, vultures, ospreys, and falcons.

American Bald Eagle

Almost all birds of prey are excellent fliers. ⟶

## Fast flier

The peregrine falcon is the fastest animal in the world. When it dives through the air from a great height, it can reach speeds of 120 mph (200 kph).

## Other birds of prey

Golden Eagle          Buzzard          Vulture

All birds of prey have very good eyesight.

A powerful, hooked beak is used for tearing meat and breaking bones.

Birds of prey have four curved claws, called talons, on each foot. They use the back talon to hold and crush their prey.

## A firm grip

Ospreys mainly eat fish. They fly over rivers, lakes, ponds, and coastlines, then dive down to the surface of the water to grab fish with their feet. Spiny scales on the osprey's feet make it easier for it to grip slippery fish.

Secretary Bird

# Seabirds

Seabirds live and feed around the world's oceans. They live onshore or high among the cliffs. They are expert hunters – gliding, swooping, and diving to catch fish.

## Frigatebird

The frigatebird cannot swim, but it has a massive wingspan and is a very skillful flier. It gets most of its food by stealing from other seabirds in the air!

Puffins are excellent swimmers and divers. They use their wings to paddle underwater and their webbed feet to steer.

Most puffins breed in underground burrows. Some burrows can be 6.5 ft (2 m) long.

The puffin is also known as the "sea parrot," because during the breeding season its beak turns a bright color.

Puffins can hold several fish in their beak at one time. They have an extra bone in their jaw that allows them to grip the fish and open their beak at the same time.

Puffin

## Pelicans

Pelicans are seabirds with a large throat sac, which they use to scoop up fish like a fishing net. They then swallow the fish whole. They can hold more fish in their beak than in their stomach.

# Birds of the rain forest

Warm, steamy rain forests are home to many strange and unusual birds that may have colorful feathers and beaks. You can find birds like hummingbirds, parrots, toucans, and cock-of-the-rock birds living in these areas of the world.

Sulphur-Breasted Toucan

Cock-of-the-Rock Bird

## Cock-of-the-rock birds

Cock-of-the-rock birds live in the rain forests of South America. Male birds have bright, striking feathers and a large crest on top of their head. In order to attract a mate, the males perform dances, at special display areas in the forest.

## Hummingbirds

Beautiful hummingbirds have
feathers that shine and change
color with the light. They are
incredible fliers and can fly
forwards, backwards,
and twist upside down,
as well as hovering
in the air to collect
nectar from flowers.

Carib
Hummingbird

## Toucans

Toucans live in Central and South
America. You can recognize a toucan by its large,
colorful beak, which can be up to one-third the length
of its body! The beak is hollow and despite its size it is
quite light. Toucans use their large beak to reach fruit
from faraway branches.

# Glossary

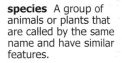

This glossary explains some of the harder words in the book.

**body feathers** The outer weatherproof feathers on a bird's body.

**crest** The feathers, bone, or fur on top of an animal's head.

**diving** To fly, fall, or jump quickly downwards through the air, sometimes into water.

**down feathers** The fluffy, soft feathers that are found underneath a bird's outer feathers. Down feathers help to keep a bird warm.

**flight feathers** The curved feathers found in a bird's wings. These feathers help a bird to fly.

**gliding** To move smoothly. Birds often glide without flapping their wings as much as normal.

**hollow** Something that is empty inside.

**hunter** An animal that looks for and kills another animal for food.

**mimic** To copy someone or something and try to act like them.

**molt** To shed feathers, fur, skin, or horns before growing a replacement.

**muscle** Something that makes an animal or human's body move.

**oxygen** A gas that we breathe in order to live. Animals also need oxygen to live.

**plume** A large, long, colorful feather.

**predator** An animal that hunts and eats other animals.

**scales** The small plates that overlap each other like roof tiles on an animal's body.

**species** A group of animals or plants that are called by the same name and have similar features.

**steer** To move in a certain direction.

**swooping** To move downwards suddenly from above.

**talon** An animal's claw.

**waterproof** Something that does not let water through.

**webbed foot** A foot where the toes are joined together by skin.

**wingspan** The distance on a bird that is usually measured from the tip of one wing to the tip of the other wing.